Overcome and Get it Done

Overcome and Get it Done

Productivity Principles that Enabled Me to Write this Book in 24 Hours

by Jamie Dixon

www.shapingpaths.com

ISBN-13: 978-1-5272-9629-9

CONTENTS

FOREWORD 1

CHAPTER ONE *THE PLEASURE PAIN PRINCIPLE* 3

CHAPTER TWO *MAKE THE FUTURE INFLUENCE THE PRESENT* 5

CHAPTER THREE *USE WILLPOWER SPARINGLY* 8

CHAPTER FOUR *CONNECT WITH YOUR UNCONSCIOUS* 11

CHAPTER FIVE *OVERCOME YOUR LIMITING BELIEFS* 14

CHAPTER SIX *PLANT SEEDS* 17

CHAPTER SEVEN *VISUALISE IDEAS BROUGHT TO LIFE* 19

CHAPTER EIGHT *MAKE HARD THINGS EASY* 21

CHAPTER NINE *CREATE ACCOUNTABILITY* 23

CHAPTER TEN *BE THE ARCHITECT OF YOUR OWN SUFFERING* .. 25

CHAPTER ELEVEN *YOUR JOB IS ALWAYS TO SERVE* 28

CHAPTER TWELVE *PERFECTIONISM IS ARROGANCE* 31

CHAPTER THIRTEEN *SURF THE WAVES OF MOTIVATION* 33

CHAPTER FOURTEEN *THINKING BREEDS INACTION* 36

CHAPTER FIFTEEN *SACRIFICE* 39

CHAPTER SIXTEEN *BATCH PROCESS* 42

CHAPTER SEVENTEEN *OUTSOURCE* 45

CHAPTER EIGHTEEN *FIND YOUR TOOL* 48

CHAPTER NINETEEN *ALWAYS START SMALL* 50

CHAPTER TWENTY *BUILD A WALL* 52

CHAPTER TWENTY-ONE *FIND THE RIGHT CONSTRAINTS* 54

CHAPTER TWENTY-TWO *REST, FUEL AND MOVE* 56

CHAPTER TWENTY-THREE *ALWAYS BE EXPERIMENTING* 58

CHAPTER TWENTY-FOUR *PERFECTION IS A PROCESS* 60

ABOUT THE AUTHOR 62

FOREWORD

WE ALL HAVE big things we've been meaning to do, but so far haven't done. Like the book we've been meaning to write, or the filing cabinets we've been meaning to sort, or the website we've been meaning to design.

Too many important tasks get put off for the wrong reasons.

This book was also one of those tasks. I'd thought for a long time that one day I should write a book about productivity. But that was always as far as the idea went. Until a month ago when a conversation with a friend sparked an idea.

We would both dedicate 24 hours to finishing something we've been meaning to do but so far haven't done. And my task would be to write, and publish, a whole new book in 24 hours.

This idea quickly turned into a movement called 24 Let's Go, which you can learn more about at 24letsgo.com. Dozens of people joined, committed and accomplished the kinds of tasks they'd been meaning to do but so far hadn't done. Some designed apps, some reorganised their life, some restructured their business.

You're reading this book now because I successfully completed my first 24 Let's Go challenge.

As I wrote it, I wanted to explore the principles that were enabling me to get it all done in just 24 hours. These are principles that have helped me overcome perfectionism and procrastination and increased my productivity. They've helped me be focused, disciplined and healthy. If you're struggling with any of these things, then I sincerely hope this book can help you find the little spark you need to make a difference.

This book is a short read. After all, I wrote it in only 24 hours, so what do you expect? But I hope it is an insightful read. I hope that as you read it you feel empowered by it. I hope it becomes the kind of book that you can pull out at any time, flip to a page at random, and find some inspiration to help you get stuff done.

Whenever you're struggling to get something done, remember: I wrote this book in just 24 hours using the principles in this very book. If I can do it, I'm sure you can too.

CHAPTER ONE

The Pleasure Pain Principle

TO GET THINGS done, of course we need to depend on motivation. Either motivation, or will power. And there is a slight difference between the two, with my preference being motivation.

To understand motivation, we need to familiarise ourselves with the Pleasure Pain Principle.

This principle states that all living beings, be they bacteria, dogs, or even human beings, are motivated by the same exact driving forces: to approach pleasure and avoid pain. Bacteria like to approach certain chemicals and avoid certain temperatures, dogs like to approach bones and avoid cats, and human beings…Well, we're a bit complicated.

We have an incredible imagination that basically enables us to time travel. Our imagination allows us to transport ourselves to the past or the future. Any time you find yourself thinking about the stupid thing you said in that meeting yesterday, or worrying about how to get through all that work tomorrow, you are basically time travelling. Our ability to do this is far superior to other species. So much so that we basically end up with two types of motivation.

The first type is all about the Present. It's all about approaching pleasure and avoiding pain in this exact moment.

The second type, though, is all about the Future. It's about our hopes and dreams of the pleasures we could get for ourselves in the future, and the pains we definitely want to avoid in the future.

Writing this book, I am motivated very strongly by the Future. Honestly speaking, I look forward to telling people that I wrote a book in 24 hours. I look forward to the pride that I will feel at having accomplished this. I also look forward to being able to say I am now the author of two books. And as I have been telling so many people over the last month that I will write a book in 24 hours, I am also motivated to avoid the humiliation (pain) of not completing this challenge!

But our Future motivation frequently comes into conflict with our Present motivation.

Right now, there are a lot of challenges I must face in order to finish writing this. I didn't sleep well last night, so at some point I will be tempted by the pleasure of a good sleep. The sun is shining and the weather is nice, after two weeks of some of the coldest temperatures I've ever experienced in Shanghai, so I will also be tempted by the pleasure of going for a stroll in the park. These temptations, or in other words, Present motivations, will conflict with my Future motivations.

How do we manage this conflict?

That is what we shall explore in the next few principles.

CHAPTER TWO

Make the Future Influence the Present

IT IS POSSIBLE to make our Future motivations so strong that they influence our motivation in the Present moment.

Between 2016 and 2018, I meditated every single day. I had an app tracking how many days in a row I had meditated for, and I got to well over 700 days.

After several hundred days of this running streak, I became afraid of losing this streak. To start all over again would have been a massive loss. The thought of that loss caused me so much panic that it drove me to meditate every day.

That wasn't a very mindful way of meditating! Thankfully my first son was born in 2018 and I had no choice but to break off, but I thought the excuse was acceptable enough! After breaking that streak, I reflected some more on how to approach my mindfulness practice in a more mindful way! I can happily say that I am no longer meditating for the numbers on an app anymore, and my meditation practice is much more relaxing than before!

The example above demonstrates an important principle; we can make our Future motivations so strong that they influence our Present motivations. The thought of losing that running streak created pain in the present moment, which motivated me to meditate.

When hope and fear generate excitement and panic in the present moment, this is a sign that our Future motivation is strong enough.

Since I've had kids, there's been a lot of hope and fear generating a lot of excitement and panic.

Expenses have suddenly increased as I must now pay for health insurance for two more people, plus various educational fees, and these will only increase. The fear of not being able to afford these has at times led to a bit of panic when work has dried up.

But kids also bring a lot of hope. I dream of lovely family holidays with them, taking them to beautiful places around the world. I also dream of being able to spend more time at home enjoying quality time with them. Then, when I think of how writing books, designing online courses, and creating new training products for my business could make those dreams a reality, I feel excitement.

Our Future motivations must be strong enough to influence our Present motivations if we are to be motivated to take purposeful actions in the present. If we don't take purposeful actions in the present moment, we will take impulsive actions. We'll scroll mindlessly through our phone, or watch cat videos, or just keep grabbing snack after snack after snack.

But we don't always need to depend on motivation to take purposeful action in the present. We can also use Willpower to do that too. And we shall explore that in the next section.

And in the coming sections we will also explore how to make our Future motivations so big that they influence our Present motivations.

CHAPTER THREE

Use Willpower Sparingly

A FANTASTIC METAPHOR to help us understand Future and Present motivations, as well as Willpower, is the Elephant and Rider Metaphor.

Picture a man riding an elephant through a forest. The man sitting on top of the elephant represents our Future motivation. He can clearly see ahead to his future destination, and gives the elephant direction on where to go. On the other hand, the elephant can only see a few feet ahead and therefore is far more concerned with what it can see in those few feet than what the rider can see in the distance.

The rider must persuade the elephant to head in the right direction. If the elephant gets off course, he could beat the elephant with a stick, or dangle bananas in front of it. By doing either of these, the future-focused rider starts to influence the present-focused elephant. This is motivation.

But there's also something else he could do.

He could get off the elephant, go behind it and push it. This is Willpower.

Willpower is the force we use to resist our Present motivations.

When you really want to eat that chocolate cake, but force yourself to eat a salad instead, that's willpower. When you really want to stop running and just go home and watch Netflix, but you force yourself to get through those next 10km, that's willpower. And when you really want to tell that horrible colleague what you really think of them, but force yourself to nod politely and fake a smile, that's willpower.

We seem to glorify willpower in our culture. But we shouldn't.

Honestly, imagine trying to push an elephant! What's going to happen? Of course you're not going to move it very far; more likely you will not move it at all and exhaust yourself just trying. This is why people burn out; because they're trying to push an elephant that doesn't want to move.

In short spurts, willpower is very useful. You may be able to get the elephant to budge a few inches. You may be able to resist the chocolate cake your colleague offers you for those thirty seconds. You may be able to run two or three kilometres on just pure willpower. You may be able to say just a few polite words to that horrible colleague using just willpower. But to do any more than that, you're going to need motivation.

With motivation, you don't have to force anything. The elephant just moves. That way, you can sit back, relax and enjoy the ride.

Ideally, we want to depend on motivation to get things done. So, while Willpower can be useful and sometimes powerful in the present, we're going to ditch Willpower here, and start exploring motivation.

CHAPTER FOUR

Connect With Your Unconscious

YOUR RIDER AND elephant, in other words your future and present selves, already want a lot of the same things anyway. It's just that they can't always see it.

There's a game I play in some of my training workshops that requires good communication skills to complete.

I split the participants into groups, and give each group a set of instructions. One group's goal is to take all of the chairs in the room and arrange them into a line. But another group's goal is to take all of the chairs in the room and arrange them into a circle.

When we start the game, both groups go around stealing chairs from each other. The first group starts putting their chairs into a line, and the other group starts stealing them and putting them into a circle.

Arguments break out, chair backs and legs are being pulled in all directions, and each team starts protecting their chairs from the other team.

But after a while, someone realises their goals are actually exactly the same. A line and a circle are the same thing. So they arrange all the chairs into a circular line and complete the game.

The exact same thing happens between our rider and elephant, or our future and present selves.

For example, I am addicted to creating stuff. I've noticed a lot of other solopreneurs like myself have exactly the same addiction. In fact, this book is an outcome of that addiction!

My future self would love a future life where I spend more time doing things I enjoy. My present self wants exactly the same thing! So here I am, writing a book!

But what I have realised recently is that instead of creating new things, I would be able to significantly increase the quality of my life if I spent more time creating value from the things I have already created. In other words, I could write more books and design more online courses, but books and online courses don't sell themselves. I need to pour my creativity into finding ways of creating more value (aka making more money) from the books and online courses I have already created.

It's easy to do the things we want to do. But we don't always realise what we need to do.

And the simplest way to discover what we need to do, to discover what aligns our future and present selves, to discover what aligns our rider and elephant, is to ask one simple question:

"What am I doing this for?"

This question plunges into our unconscious. It surfaces the needs buried deep in our mind that we hadn't realised were there.

If you're spending too much time on your phone, then what are you doing that for? If you're being too strict on your kids, then what are you doing that for? If you're getting involved in endless political debates, then what are you doing that for?

"What am I doing this for?" will reveal the motivations that your future and present selves already have in common, and the future or present motivation you already have.

CHAPTER FIVE

Overcome Your Limiting Beliefs

WHEN YOUR FUTURE and present motivations are connected but conflicting with each other, it's normally a sign that you have limiting beliefs.

Limiting beliefs are basically the beliefs we hold about the way the world works that create problems for us.

For example, there are many people in the corporate world who believe they cannot say "No" to senior leaders.

Their present motivation is to please these senior leaders. But this conflicts with their future motivation of wanting to please these senior leaders, because as they say "Yes" to too many tasks, they become overwhelmed and can't deliver on what they promised.

The problem here is that they believe they cannot say "No" to senior leaders. So whenever a senior leader asks them to do something, this results in their behaviour of saying "Yes".

Beliefs create behaviour.

It's a little bit like carpet and floorboards. If the floorboard is rotten, then laying new carpet on it won't solve the problem. We shouldn't just change behaviour without altering the underlying beliefs.

So to address limiting beliefs, we can follow a 4 step process:

Step 1: What problems am I facing right now?

Problems are normally an indicator of limiting beliefs. If you've ended up with too many work tasks then that's probably a symptom of having a limiting belief.

Step 2: What limiting beliefs may have caused those problems?

If I have too much work, it's probably because of my belief that I cannot say "No".

Step 3: Redefine those limiting beliefs into success beliefs.

Now turn that limiting belief of 'I cannot say "No" to senior leaders' into a success belief of 'I can propose alternative suggestions to their requests'.

Step 4: Imagine and practise new behaviours that align with the success beliefs.

If I now believe that I can propose alternative suggestions to their requests, then the new behaviour that comes with this may involve asking these senior leaders lots of questions to understand their underlying needs, and then proposing alternative suggestions.

A lot of our limiting beliefs are contextual as well. In other words, they serve us in some contexts, and only become limiting beliefs in other contexts. The limiting belief of not being able to say "No" to senior leaders may have served us well at school with our strict teachers, but doesn't serve us well in the modern working world.

When addressing limiting beliefs, you may find some problems are built on top of multiple limiting beliefs, and we need to redefine each of those into success beliefs, and imagine and practise new behaviours to align with those new success beliefs.

When we do redefine new success beliefs, it's as if we have blinkers suddenly removed from our eyes. All of a sudden, we can see a much broader world, with a greater range of possibilities.

CHAPTER SIX

Plant Seeds

SO FAR WE'VE looked at several ways of finding the driving force to get things done. We could use willpower, although ideally we want to use that sparingly. Or we could connect with our unconscious by asking "What am I doing this for?" to find how our present and future motivations are already aligned. Or we could redefine our limiting beliefs to success beliefs, to remove the blinders from our eyes, and open us up to new and more effective ways of getting things done.

But now, let's go back to an idea we looked at earlier: making the future influence the present.

When we want to make an effort to change our motivation, we can start doing so by planting seeds.

The idea of writing this book started with a conversation with my good friend Joeri at The Magic Sauce. I explained to him that it took me six years to write my first book. Then last year I started work on my second book (which thanks to this one will now become my third book!) and it took me only six months to complete the first draft. Then he challenged me. He said, "You've learned a lot about how to get things done faster – why don't you turn that into an online course?".

And thus, a seed was planted.

So I upped the stakes and said, "I could totally write a book in 24 hours!".

That was over a month ago now. Since then, this seed has grown. I started to dream about this book. Ideas started bubbling up in my mind. I was excited. I told everyone I could about what I was going to do.

As this seed grew stronger and stronger, the future motivation of completing this book started to overpower any present motivations I had. I became fixated on finding ways of clearing my schedule so I could focus on this. I hunted for hotels in the right location so I could find a quiet space to work. I prepared as best I could.

Seeds can be planted in conversations, but they can also be planted in other ways.

One of the best ways is to simply write things down.

When I write things down in my To Do list and process them, 90% of those things get done. When I pencil in time on my calendar to do things, 100% of those things get done.

A seed may start as an idea. But it needs fertile soil to be planted in, and it needs that fertile soil soon. How do we create that fertile soil? When we start planning, scheduling, and making space in the world for our idea to come to life, we create the fertile soil. And when we start turning this idea into a tangible thing that we and other people can see, hear, smell, taste or touch, then the seed grows bigger. At some point, that seed becomes a tree, and our future motivation starts to overpower our present motivation.

CHAPTER SEVEN

Visualise Ideas Brought to Life

WHEN WE SETTLE on an idea to do something, the goal then becomes making this a reality.

Ideas exist only in our mind. The amazing thing about our mind is that we can use our imagination to create things that have never existed.

Once upon a time, farms did not exist, and then the agricultural revolution happened. Once upon a time, rockets did not exist, and then the space race happened. Once upon a time, iPhones did not exist, and then Steve Jobs happened.

This is something other species can't do. Other species live in the real world. They can only follow the rules of the real world. But we have broken free from the real world, and can create new worlds in our imaginations.

But of course, the real world is still what matters.

Everyone has ideas. But most people don't act on their ideas. If you want to use your God- given gift of being able to alter reality, then you need to turn those ideas into reality.

The first place to start is through visualisation.

Visualisation is where our mind connects with our senses. Our mind is separated from the real world by a grey blob of brain matter sitting inside a dark skull. But it is connected to reality through our senses. The data we receive through our eyes, ears, mouth, nose, skin, etc. tell our mind what the real world is like, and our mind works with that data to make sense of it all.

Our mind already has a massive library of sensory experiences which it uses to represent ideas. You can easily visualise what a dog looks like, or imagine the smell of chocolate cake with pumpkin spice, or even feel your ears popping as you imagine going up a lift in a tall skyscraper.

If you want to bring your ideas to life, then start by using your library of sensory representations to imagine what this idea will be like. Visualise your ideas brought to life.

If you brought this idea to life then what would you see, hear, smell, taste or feel?

The clearer this sensory representation in your mind is, the far more certain and confident you will feel about it, because you will know that this could become a reality. It could become something you can see, hear, smell, taste or touch in the tangible, real world.

The confidence that comes with that will drive you. You'll stop second guessing yourself, you'll stop wondering if it can be done, and you'll start feeling excited about the possibilities you could bring into the world. You'll go from worrying about how to make it happen, to thinking about how to make it awesome.

You are a human being. You have been born with the God-given ability to change reality. Use it wisely.

CHAPTER EIGHT

Make Hard Things Easy

YES, WE WANT to make our future motivation so strong that it influences the present. But we must not forget the constraints of our present motivations. It is after all our present motivations that are the elephant that will carry our rider to his destination. Our present motivation is what we must depend upon to do all the heavy lifting that our future motivation requires.

Like an elephant that can only see a few feet ahead of it, our present motivation is only focused on approaching pleasure and avoiding pain in this exact moment.

Whilst we may have done a great job of ensuring our future and present motivations are aligned, we mustn't get carried away. There is one specific constraint that we must keep in mind at all times, and it goes back to the pleasure-pain principle.

If something is too painful to even think about, let alone do, then we won't do it.

I'm not much of a runner. I enjoy calisthenics and yoga, but running is not my thing. So, if you challenged me to run 20km, I'd probably tell you to go do something unpleasant to yourself.

If instead you challenged me to run 500 metres, I'd probably be up for that.

And then once I complete the 500 metres, you could totally manipulate me, and challenge me to run another 500 metres.

With enough small and easy milestones covered, you may eventually be able to convince me to run a full 20km.

People don't do big things. Big things involve too much pain.

But big things are made up of lots of baby steps, and people like baby steps.

Baby steps require no pain whatsoever, and they're not even painful to think about. Furthermore, if each baby step has a reward, even the reward of knowing that you've just got a lot closer to your overall goal, then we super-like those kinds of baby steps.

To bring your new idea to life, whatever it may be, probably involves quite a lot of steps. The smaller you can make each of those steps, the faster you will accomplish it.

Those baby steps should be so easy to do that they require no thinking whatsoever. And then, as you progress through each baby step, you'll find the sense of achievement increases your confidence, which will push you through even further. At some point, you'll realise you're so close to the end that you will not be able to think of anything else but completing it.

And so, on that note, I've just hit my first milestone for this book. So, I'm going to reward myself with a nice lunch break. Be back shortly!

CHAPTER NINE

Create Accountability

FOR SOME THINGS, we just don't hold ourselves accountable. Because why should we? If we don't hit our targets, then it's far easier to change our targets than it is to punish ourselves!

Accountability is when we invite other people to provide us with pleasures to seek and pains to avoid. It's generally more effective when we invite other people to give us pleasures to seek and pains to avoid, because we can't control the pleasures and pains they bring our way!

At the very least, they can nag us. Checking in on us every so often to make sure we're doing what we said we were going to do, and if we're not then they can give us a good telling off. At the very least, they can bring an annoyance that then becomes a pain we want to avoid.

Slightly above nagging is shame. Shame is always a social thing. If we don't do what we said we'd do, then we lose their respect, and they may even share their lack of respect for us with other people, and we lose respect amongst even more people. We generally don't like shame, so that becomes a pain to avoid.

They may even reward us. This is why having a boss helps a lot with motivation, because they can either promote us and give us a pay rise (pleasure!) or fire us and remove our financial security (pain!).

So, when it's time to take action, a great way to create Present motivation that aligns with our Future motivation is to create accountability.

Perhaps we can ask a friend to check in with us.

Perhaps we can make a very public commitment that would be extremely embarrassing not to live up to! Social media helps immensely with this. It especially helps if we make this public commitment multiple times so that it is kept very clearly in everyone's minds.

Or perhaps we could even go as far as to give someone a large sum of money, and tell them that if we do not live up to this commitment then they can keep that money for themselves, or if we do then they give us our money back.

Accountability is a great way of manipulating your own motivation.

And you absolutely should manipulate your own motivation. If you've got BIG goals, you NEED motivation to achieve them. Waiting for motivation to come is like waiting for aliens to land in your back yard. It's extremely unlikely to happen. You need to actively start shaping your motivation, and creating accountability is one of the best ways to do that.

CHAPTER TEN

Be The Architect Of Your Own Suffering

IN LIFE, THERE is suffering. We cannot escape this fact.

The most successful business people you can think of suffer. The happiest person you know suffers. Even those Instagram influencers showing off their amazing fake lives suffer too.

Suffering comes when we are either pulled away, or intentionally move away, from the pleasures we seek in the current moment.

Want job security? Well, you're fired! Want chocolate cake? Sorry, you're now a diabetic. Want a productive morning routine with meditation, yoga and journaling? Ha, now you're a parent!

But I strongly believe that suffering on our own terms is way better than suffering at the hands of something we cannot control. And because of that, I believe we SHOULD intentionally create our own suffering.

In my career as a coach and trainer, I have come across a few too many people who have been too comfortable in their jobs for too long. They turn up to work, they go through the motions, they go home. Maybe due to their own limiting beliefs they stopped growing ages ago, or maybe this job just doesn't allow them the room to grow anymore, or maybe they simply lack accountability and this negatively affects their motivation. But for whatever reason, they've stopped growing and they are left in a state of comfort.

If you are one of these people, you should be scared.

Every so often, the economy likes to take these kinds of people and throw them off a cliff.

When times get tough, the ones who have a refined ability for adapting to change survive, while those who have forgotten how to adapt die.

If you have been enjoying a comfortable period of time for a few days, a few weeks, even a few months, then by all means enjoy that time. Periods of comfort in life can be rare, and they are a blessing.

But once that comfortable period of time extends beyond a few years, you are in serious danger.

When you realise you are in the danger zone, you have two options.

You can either wait for fate to torture you.

Or you can torture yourself.

But if you wait for fate to torture you, you don't know how bad it's going to be.

When you choose to torture yourself, you can control that. You can take baby steps. You can take a break. You can keep your safety net.

Have you been living in the same country for too long? Then start teaching yourself a new language or culture before globalisation catches up with you.

Have you been allowing yourself to get dangerously overweight? Then exercise and diet before heart disease catches up with you.

Have you been working in the same company longer than anyone else you know? Then quickly change jobs, and – hell, why not? – industries, while you're at it, before the company restructures and renders you redundant.

In life there is suffering. You can either wait for it to happen to you, or create it on your own terms. I prefer the latter.

CHAPTER ELEVEN

Your Job is Always to Serve

WE TEND TO think of ourselves as a highly competitive, territorial, tribal species. Because all around us we see proof of this. We see political divides, national divides, corporations competing with each other and so on. It would be easy to think that we are an extremely selfish species.

But it is equally easy to see that we are actually an extremely cooperative species.

Just consider the lunch that I had today. I paid the waiters with my own money, and they rewarded me with food. The restaurant paid the waiters their salary, and they rewarded the restaurant with their time. The restaurant paid its vendors their fees, and they rewarded it with all the resources it needs to operate.

The entire world economy depends upon human cooperation.

The very computer I am using is a symbol of that. Consider all of the designers, manufacturers, raw material providers, logistics companies, financial consulting services, retail training companies and so on that were involved in this. Even simple things like the pigments that make up the colours of my keyboard keys, or the raw materials the CPU is made of, or how an entire operating system can work on such a piece of hardware, all have incredible stories of human cooperation behind them.

Money does not make the world go round. Cooperation does.

And if you want to be a valued part of this incredible miracle of human cooperation, then you need to play your role in it. The key is to realise that your job is always to serve other people, no matter what you do.

Your job is not to follow orders. It's not to meet the required standards. It's not to tick boxes. It's to serve people.

Even if your job is to stamp pieces of paper, who are you doing that for? How could you be of better service to them? Maybe you could find a way of reducing the amount of paperwork they must read, for which they will be very grateful!

Even if your job is to pour cups of coffee, who are you doing that for? How could you be of better service to them? Maybe you could spare a few seconds to ask them how their day has been so far, and be the one person that's listened to them all morning.

Even if your job is to assemble parts in a factory, who are you doing that for? How could you be of better service to them? Maybe you can see a much more efficient way of arranging the assembly line that would save the company a lot of money and time.

It is the people who get clear on who they are serving, and find ways of serving them better, that get the best opportunities in life.

Service is the most meaningful form of accountability.

CHAPTER TWELVE

Perfectionism Is Arrogance

WHEN IT COMES to serving other people, our own standards don't really matter. It's the standards of the people we serve that matter.

I almost didn't publish my first book. I'd spent six years on it already, and I still wasn't satisfied. There were parts I wanted to redo, there were things I wish I hadn't written, and some extra things I thought I should have written. But I gave myself a deadline, and used accountability to make that deadline very motivating, and eventually I got it out there.

I was pleasantly surprised when people started reaching out to me months later saying how much they had enjoyed my book. Despite all the internal criticisms I'd had, these people enjoyed it and found it useful.

I learned an important lesson from this. What I thought about it didn't really matter. Ultimately, the book was for them, the readers, not for me.

As I am writing this book, I am not even giving myself the time to criticise it. I know it's not going to be perfect. But I also know it will never be perfect, because what the hell is perfect anyway?

When we use our own self-doubts to stop ourselves from sharing our creative work with the rest of the world, we're making it about us, when it should be about them.

It is better to release a little at a time, get feedback from the people we're meant to serve, and then adapt accordingly. If we're serving them, then their standards matter, so we'd better learn what their standards are!

For another book I am writing, I have been sharing each section on social media as I publish it on my blog. I have several dozen people following this blog, and every so often some of them will reach out to tell me what they like and what they don't like. That way, I learn what their standards are and I adapt.

When perfectionism holds us back, it's because we value our own standards too highly. We've decided that what we think is what matters.

Of course, there may be certain standards that matter to us that we should hold onto. For example, in my work as a trainer, I care more about sustainable behaviour change than classroom engagement. I'm willing to sacrifice fun and games if I think other things will lead to better chances of sustainable behaviour change. Sometimes people tell me they thought my training was fun, when I thought it was ineffective. Other times they tell me they thought it could have been more engaging, when I thought it was effective. And yes, that's still selfish of me. But I consciously chose those standards because I want to serve people who care about effectiveness and not people who care about fun and games.

So it is important to get clear on who we serve, or who we want to serve, and use their standards as the benchmark for success. Perfectionism is a barrier to serving them.

CHAPTER THIRTEEN

Surf the Waves of Motivation

IN THE PREVIOUS few principles, we've explored how we can shape our own motivation, and use accountability to do so. But there's also another thing we can do with motivation.

Motivation is always fluctuating, because the world around us, and within us, is always changing.

On June 22nd, 2018, I was extremely motivated to go and join a few friends I hadn't seen for a long time and play board games with them. But then, as I was getting ready to head out, my wife went into labour with our first son! My motivation completely changed!

Naturally, my friends were very understanding. Having my first son was a good enough excuse not to catch up with them!

The above is an extreme example of how our motivation can fluctuate. And whilst that was a pretty big example, we experience frequent fluctuations on a small and large scale on a daily basis.

Perhaps we wake up feeling sick, and now we don't have the motivation to go to the gym anymore. Maybe we got stuck in traffic for two hours with no food, so when we see the cake shop our motivation to stick to that diet goes out of the window. Maybe we ate something bad, and as we're giving an important presentation to a group of potential clients, our motivation to rush off to the bathroom takes over!

Motivation fluctuates all the time. Think of it like a wave. It comes and goes. At certain times of the day and under certain conditions it is stronger or weaker. The better you get at surfing that wave, the easier you will find it to take purposeful actions and achieve meaningful goals.

So learn about your wave.

What is it that you want to do? Do you want to go running? Do you want to write a book? Do you want to spend quality time with your children?

Then ask, for that action, when is your motivation wave at its peak and when is it at its trough?

Then ask, what action could I take to influence these peaks and troughs?

When it comes to writing, I know my motivation wave very well. I know I am more motivated to write during the daytime, and not at all during the night-time. I know I need a dedicated space, either somewhere quiet like a library, or somewhere with reasonable background noise like a cafe. I know I need the right kind of music to help me concentrate. I know what kinds of food will sustain me.

Serving the waves of motivation is such an effective way of getting things done. Learn about your waves, find out when the peaks and troughs come, and how to influence those peaks and troughs. And then plan your actions to coincide with those peaks and troughs.

CHAPTER FOURTEEN

Thinking Breeds Inaction

AS I AM writing this book, I find myself hitting a flow. I'm getting through it much faster than I thought I would, and probably the main reason is because I am not stopping to think.

Now, I'm not going to completely discredit thinking here. I love thinking. I thoroughly enjoyed spending six years thinking about my first book! And thinking things through in depth has led to a lot of my greatest ideas, and enables me to articulate things to people in clear and concise ways.

But when it comes to action, thinking needs to stop.

Yes, there is a time for thinking. That time is both before and after action.

But when it comes to action, thinking needs to stop.

Because as we think, we give room for our limiting beliefs, for our self-critic, for doubts to plant their seeds and grow strong. We start to doubt ourselves, we start to question what we're doing, we start to consider what else we should be doing. All of this breeds inaction.

I say I am writing this book in 24 hours, but really, it's taken me 35 years to write this book. A lot of what I'm writing about are ideas that I've thought of before. I've trained people on them, I've reflected on them, I've debated them.

So these ideas are not new to me. They've just been buried deep in my mind, and I've needed time to dig them out.

And because I've done that thinking before, I am now qualified to take action in this very moment.

There will be mistakes. My grammar will be a bit off. I may write some things that I eventually disagree with! There may be things that I could have written in a better way. But I can take care of all those things AFTER I write, when I can start thinking again.

Right now is simply time for action.

Here's a fun game you can play to test your ability to act on the spot. Look around you right now, and choose the first object you see. Now, speaking out loud, tell a story about it. Don't stop, don't try to think of anything better, don't edit yourself, just tell a story about it.

It will probably be a ridiculous story. It probably won't make any sense whatsoever. But that doesn't matter. What matters is your ability to shut off the critical voices in your mind as you are doing that and just focus on that one thing.

This is something I have started practising with my two-year-old son at bed time. Although he's only two years old, I am amazed at his ability to tell stories without thinking. Sure, they don't make any sense whatsoever! But he has zero critical filters right now, and mastering the ability to shut off his critical filters will be of great help to him when it comes to getting things done.

And shutting off my critical filters has helped get this done.

CHAPTER FIFTEEN

Sacrifice

GETTING THINGS DONE is actually a lot more about choosing what not to get done.

To write this book, I've sacrificed two nights away from my family. I've sacrificed all the other tasks I could be working on right now. I've sacrificed video games, working out and reading.

One of the biggest killers of productivity is not sacrificing enough.

We only have so much energy, so much time and so many resources. There are so, so, so many things we could do with all of these. The biggest question is not what we should do, but what we shouldn't do.

If you have something important to get done right now, then what do you need to sacrifice?

Is it time? Is it money? Is it energy? Something else?

Most people have too many commitments in this modern world. Our minds simply can't cope with that.

They're literally not designed to, either. Try this experiment…

Think of the capital city of your home country and spell it out loud. Now think of the name of the last shop you bought something from and spell that out loud. Easy, right?

Now, spell both those things at the same time, one letter after another. So if it's Beijing and Starbucks then you would spell B-S-e-t-i-a etc.

That's hard, right?

The reason is because your brain can't process those two things at once.

Think of it like an old computer loading up a bloated piece of software. Spelling the capital city of your home country requires loading up one piece of software, but spelling the name of the last shop you bought something from requires loading up another piece of software.

It's OK if we load up one piece of software, use it, then close it down when we're finished. But when we load up one software, use it a bit, then close it down and load up another, use that a bit, then close that down and load up the other again, this is incredibly inefficient. You can imagine the whirring sounds that old computer would make.

But we do this on a daily basis. It is a massive waste of energy. We are literally leaking cognitive energy. And that's because we place too high demands on our cognitive systems.

The solution is straightforward. Sacrifice anything non-essential. Spend as long as you can focusing on just one thing.

I know it's not always possible. Some jobs make it almost impossible to focus, and some sacrifices just aren't practical. But there are some other ways to gain focus, and we'll look at those in the next few sections.

CHAPTER SIXTEEN

Batch Process

IN THE LAST section, I gave the analogy of an old computer loading up a bloated piece of software.

Think of each task as following under a certain category of software. There are analytical tasks, creative tasks, administrative tasks and so on.

When we start a task of that category, our brain needs to load up the right software for that task.

Loading up that software takes time. It may be a few seconds, it may be a few minutes, it may be even longer. For me when it comes to writing, I have to load up my brain's writing software. It can take me at least five minutes, and sometimes up to fifteen minutes before that software is fully loaded up.

As that software is opening up, your brain is warming up to that type of task. That warm up time means your brain is not operating at 100% effectiveness. It may only be 15%, or 60%. But to get to 100% effectiveness takes time.

So, consider what would happen if I were to write this section, and then edit it. I would require a few minutes to load up my writing software. After about 5 minutes my brain would finally be operating at 100% effectiveness. But then when I switch to editing mode, I shut down my writing software and load up my editing software. I now need to wait for that software to hit 100% effectiveness, and that will take time. And if after editing I then moved on to writing the next section, just think how much time I would have wasted!

It is much more effective to keep one type of software open once we've already opened it. We want to spend as much time as possible operating at 100% effectiveness. And this is why we should batch process.

Batch processing is where we process just one type of task in a set period of time.

What I am attempting with this book is batch processing. I have dedicated about eight hours today to just writing and nothing else.

Of course, I am taking breaks. It's also good to switch our computers, and ourselves, off from time to time and let them cool down and recover.

But when I am working, I am processing one type of task only. Once I have finished all of my writing, then I will move on to editing. Once I have finished all my editing, then I will move on to formatting.

Another task that I do this for is meetings. Meetings are a real drain of time, especially when we must travel around to get to each meeting. So I set aside one day each week as my meeting day. I book all of my meetings for just that one day. I don't do any other work on that day. It saves me a huge amount of time and energy.

So to make the most of your energy, and spend more time in peak productivity mode, process similar tasks in batches.

CHAPTER SEVENTEEN

Outsource

ANOTHER WAY OF focusing is to outsource certain tasks.

So I'm actually not going to be doing any editing. I've outsourced my editing work so that I can just focus on writing (thank you Patrick by the way for taking care of the editing for me!).

There are some things we're good at and some things we're bad at.

There are some things we want to do and some things we don't want to do.

And there are some things we need to do and some things we don't need to do.

Thankfully, we don't have to do everything. It's a big wide world, and thanks to the wonders of the internet it has never been easier to find someone to take care of the stuff you don't want to.

I will say this though; it's good to try new things. I have tried my hand at web design, copywriting, graphic design, illustration, coding and so on. I've learnt a good few things along the way. There are even some simple tasks that I could complete entirely on my own. And when I do outsource work, having some knowledge of that field of work helps me understand what they're doing and communicate with them more effectively.

But when it comes to getting stuff done, outsourcing helps you focus.

When it comes to outsourcing, you can frame your job requirements using the following framework that I call The Delegatables:

What:

The output or deliverables

Why:

The benefits of doing this task, or the compensation for doing so

How:

The methodology for completing this task

When:

The milestones and deadlines for this task

There may be certain Delegatables that you want to define, and there may be some you are comfortable letting the person you outsource to define. For example, you probably want to define the output or deliverables, but may be comfortable letting the other person decide on the methodology.

And the more freedom you give the other person to define the task, the more motivated they will be to complete the task. For example, if you give them very specific descriptions for all of the Delegatables, then they may feel very restricted. But if you allow them to decide on the compensation, methodology and even the deadlines, then they may feel more ownership of this task.

But of course, this should all be done within reason. If you are outsourcing a task, it is, at the end of the day, your task to begin with.

The goal is simply to outsource what we don't want to do, so that we can focus more on what we want to do. And ideally, we outsource in a way that motivates the other person as much as possible.

CHAPTER EIGHTEEN

Find Your Tool

ANOTHER WAY OF focusing is by using tools.

For example, I'm writing a book. I could literally write everything down on a piece of paper. I'd need a pen and paper for that. Pen and paper are tools.

But they're not the best tools for me. I'm a digital guy, in a digital age. I hate writing by hand.

So, I could use Microsoft Word. But when it comes to writing books, that is extremely clunky. So I don't use Microsoft Word.

Thankfully, there is a whole bunch of applications out there designed specifically for writing books. One of those is Scrivener, which is the app I'm using right now.

I could use other similar apps, but Scrivener is MY app. I like using it. It works in the way I want it to work. I know how to use it. I feel in harmony with Scrivener, a lot like how ancient warriors felt as one with their swords.

Tools help us do things we couldn't do before, like how airplanes enable us to fly across continents and oceans, which we literally could not do before they existed.

Tools also help us do things better than we could do before, like how jumbo jets can transport more people further and faster than the planes the Wright Brothers first flew.

Tools should also give us freedom. They should free us from the mundane tasks we don't want or need to do anymore. They shouldn't get in the way. They should just work the exact way we want them to work.

I have filled my life with a bunch of tools that I use for specific purposes. I have my iPad Pro for writing notes. I have my Neuland marker pens that I use for working on flip charts in training rooms. I have Zoom for virtual workshops. I have my Blue Yeti microphone for voiccovers.

It can take some time to find the right tools. Sometimes we need to try a few before we find the one that fits.

There is normally a learning curve involved as well.

But once we find and master our tool, it gives us freedom. The freedom to focus on JUST creating.

CHAPTER NINETEEN

Always Start Small

I USED TO procrastinate on processing my monthly expenses.

I'd go on business trips all around the country, working with a variety of partners and clients, and finish with a bulging wallet full of receipts. The sight of the thick wad of receipts did not excite me with thoughts of how much money I could get reimbursed. Instead it filled me with dread at the thought of the boring Excel spreadsheets I'd have to work through.

But I found a simple solution to this procrastination. All I had to do was get the receipts out of my wallet and put them down on my desk.

This was just the first tiny step of this mundane task. But there was nothing hard or painful about this step. And so I got it done.

Then the next thing I had to do was arrange them in date order. That took me several minutes, then I was done.

Then the next thing I had to do was open up a spreadsheet and start inputting. This was a much bigger task, but I also found a way of making this smaller. I would only spend a maximum of ten minutes on this task.

Knowing I could stop it after ten minutes allowed me to empty my mind of all the negative thoughts associated with this task. I could then focus on taking action without any thinking. And surprisingly, when I hit ten minutes I discovered I had accomplished a lot more than I thought I would.

The simplest way to overcoming procrastination is to start small. Start with the smallest possible action there is, or spend a manageable amount of time (e.g. ten minutes) on that task. And if you want to take a break after that, then that's fine, because you've already made progress and you deserve it!

When I sit down to write this book after a break, I must start small. I can't dive straight into the writing. I first start by rereading the previous two sections to get my thinking back on track. Then as soon as ideas start to emerge, I write them down. And then I suddenly find I've finished an entire section.

Never start big. Always start small. Remember, people don't do big things. We do tiny things. But a lot of tiny things eventually lead to big things.

CHAPTER TWENTY

Build a Wall

ANOTHER WAY OF focusing is to build walls around you.

We live in a world full of people. Thanks to technology, the world is even more full of people now! They live in our pockets, in our hands and on our bedside tables.

At any one moment, a person in our physical environment, or even somewhere on the other side of the planet, may distract us from focusing. It could be a toddler throwing a tantrum, it could be an automated call from a robotic advertising system, or a notification that someone liked something you posted earlier.

You know the solution to this already. Cut them off.

To write this book, I have locked myself away in a hotel room. I have two young children at home who create a wide range of distractions. My wife has been extremely supportive, and thankfully has her parents to help out whilst I'm away.

I've also switched off my phone, closed my web browser and emails and hung a "Do Not Disturb" sign on my hotel room door. So far, it's worked pretty well!

Sometimes building these walls takes a bit of preparation and communication beforehand. And when distractions do arise, it can require a good deal of ruthlessness to build our walls back up again.

When you need to focus, make a habit of telling the people in your world that you are not to be disturbed during your focus time. Make it extra obvious as well. For example, I had a colleague who used to place a toy axe on his desk whenever he needed to focus!

You may even need to find a specific location that becomes your focus location. For me it's a Costa Coffee five minutes' walk from my home. No one disturbs me there and I get a lot of stuff done! But for super focus sessions like today, it's got to be a quiet hotel room. What's your focus location?

And when distractions do emerge, be direct. Tell people you are focusing right now, tell them why you need to focus right now, tell them who else might be able to help them right now, and tell them when you will be able to help them again. Even better, prepare this script before your focus session so that you don't need to waste precious cognitive resources thinking about it.

When you need to focus, build a wall around you. When distractions break through, destroy them and then rebuild your wall.

CHAPTER TWENTY-ONE

Find the Right Constraints

WHEN IT COMES to creative work, we can apply our creative energy in one of two ways: either creating the constraints for this project, or creating within those constraints.

For example, for this book I have decided that I will stop writing around the 10,000 word mark, and that I am writing about Productivity Principles only, and that each principle will include a section no longer than 500 words. These are the constraints of this project.

I actually decided on those constraints before I started this project. So when I sat down to write today, I could instead direct my creative energy towards writing within those constraints.

If I didn't have those constraints in place already, I would have to direct my creative energy towards creating and recreating those constraints each time I started to write something new.

A good example is a PowerPoint slide. Imagine you have a blank slide and you want to add a bit of text and a photograph. If you didn't have any constraints for your slide design, you would spend ages figuring out where to put the photo and text, and which font you wanted for the text, and which colour and size and so on. You'd probably try multiple arrangements, and waste a lot of time and creative energy on figuring out these constraints.

But if instead you decided that each slide would be one large photo as the background, with a maximum of 12 words that you put on the most spacious area of the photo, then you wouldn't need to think about that again.

Haiku poems are a great example of constraints. There are three lines in total. The first line is five syllables, the second line is seven syllables and the third line is five syllables. Every single Haiku poem follows these exact constraints. And there are infinite possibilities with what you can create in a Haiku poem.

Before you start any creative project, decide on the constraints of this project. You only need to decide on the constraints ONCE. You only need to apply your creative energy to designing these constraints ONCE. And then with those constraints in place, you can now direct all your creative energy to bringing your idea to life within those exact constraints.

You could break the constraints every so often if you wanted to. Maybe you are writing a Haiku poem and feel that one more line for this poem would make it so much better. This is probably the highest level of creativity: knowing when to break the constraints.

But always use the constraints as a starting point and as a guide. Only ever break the constraints when you have a clear purpose. Always break mindfully, never mindlessly.

CHAPTER TWENTY-TWO

Rest, Fuel and Move

TODAY, AS WELL as writing this book, I have spent an hour and a half talking to other people who are taking part in this "24 Let's Go Challenge". I've posted a few things on social media, I've responded to a few messages and emails, I've gone for a walk outside, I've sat in a cafe, I've had a thirty-minute nap, I've been to the bathroom several times, I've made three cups of coffee and four cups of tea, and I have stopped more times than I can count to do some light yoga and then stare out of the window for several minutes.

I would not have been able to manage this much writing if I had not done all of the above. I need a break. We all need breaks.

Focusing on one task is exactly the same as long distance running. You need to pace yourself. Whilst you can't physically see the wear and tear being caused, that doesn't mean there is no wear and tear.

A healthy body will create a healthy mind. If I had filled my belly with junk food today, I would have been sleepy a lot earlier on. If I hadn't moved and done some light yoga, my neck would be in a lot of pain and my buttocks would be dead right now. If I hadn't gone for a walk in the sun earlier on, I'd probably be quite miserable right now.

Resting, fuelling and moving are essential for productivity. Without the right rest, fuel and movement in your life, you will not reach your optimum productivity. Someone better rested, better fuelled and better moved than you will go on to achieve much more with their creativity.

You have a body, whether you like it or not. If you don't take care of it, it won't take care of you.

CHAPTER TWENTY-THREE

Always be Experimenting

EVERYTHING WE ARE able to do is because of our neural pathways. Drinking a cup of coffee, typing on a laptop and reading a book are all things you can do because your body has the neural pathways required to do them.

Neural pathways are a lot like city streets viewed from space at night time. They're long streaks of light, some well-travelled, others less so.

When we learn to do something new, we build new neural pathways. The more neural pathways we have, the more stuff we can do. The more stuff we can do, the more productive we can be.

This is why I strongly believe in always experimenting. Try new things, do new things, do old things in new ways. When we do so, we create new neural pathways and expand our capabilities.

But a new neural pathway is like a path in a grassy field. When we tread it once, we can see the trace, but after a short while the grass folds back and the path disappears. The more we tread this path, the deeper it will be.

A lot of the things we try, we'll probably never try again. But it's only by trying new things that we can possibly discover the new neural pathways that we want to tread deeply.

Never spoken in public before? Try it. Never designed a website before? Try it. Never had a cold shower before? Try it. Never attended an online networking event before? Try it. Never created an online course before? Try it.

If you never try, you'll never know.

And if you do try, you'll eventually find new abilities.

This book is also possible because of the number of things that I have tried before. I've tried writing before. I've tried publishing before. I've tried designing training on productivity before. I've tried networking on social media before. I've tried a whole bunch of productivity techniques before. If I hadn't tried all those things, I wouldn't be able to write this book.

You have every reason to try new things, and no reasons not to.

CHAPTER TWENTY-FOUR

Perfection is a Process

I STARTED THIS book at 10:00. As I type this, it is now 19:02. Nine hours, and 10,000 words. I hit my goal. I am pleased. I am proud.

I know this book is not perfect. It shouldn't be. Neither you nor I have any right to expect it to be. I wrote, edited and published it in 24 hours after all.

But one of my reasons for writing this book is to show that we can achieve so much more when we drop the perfectionism. Done is better than perfect. Don't let perfection be the enemy of good.

And besides, perfection is not a result.

Perfection is a process.

After I write this, I will edit this. I will then give this away for free for the first month. I will collect feedback from people, which I will then use to edit the 2nd edition. I'll ask people who've read it what they think I should charge for it, or if they think I should charge for it. I'll ask people what else they think I should do with this.

The bulk of the work is now done. I've written my first draft. Now it's time to refine. And it is through constant refinement that a better output will be shaped.

Perfection is never the outcome.

Perfection is a process.

ABOUT THE AUTHOR

Hi, I'm Jamie, and thank you for reading my book.

I am a coach, trainer and author.

My mission is to help people make the impact they crave. I love working with people who see a change that needs to happen, big or small, and need to find a way of making it happen.

I care about value. Value to me is nothing to do with numbers. It's all about impacting the people we serve. Training and coaching are not the solutions I provide, they are simply mediums through which I serve people.

I believe that value and service are what makes the human world go round. The more we are able to impact others in a meaningful way, the more meaningful our own lives become.

Serving the right people is what makes my life meaningful.

I've worked with over 140 multinational companies throughout the APAC region. I work in both English and Mandarin. I am the founder of Shaping Paths, a performance consultancy that provides coaching and training for multinational companies using my unique Shaping Paths approach based on my previous book "Shaping Paths - How to Design and Deliver PRACTICAL Training".

I am originally from Mid-Sussex in the UK, and have been based in Shanghai, China for over a decade.

You can learn more about me at www.shapingpaths.com, and feel free to reach out to me directly at jamie.dixon@shapingpaths.com.

www.ingramcontent.com/pod-product-compliance
Ingram Content Group UK Ltd.
Pitfield, Milton Keynes, MK11 3LW, UK
UKHW020416250726
13967UKWH00007B/2668

9 781527 296299